Lake Country School
Montessori Learning Environments
3755 Pleasant Av. S.
Minneapolis. MN 55409

Lake Country School
Montessori Learning Environments
3755 Pleasant Av. S.
Minneapolis. MN 55409

Her Piano Sang

Her Piano Sang

A Story about
Clara Schumann

by Barbara Allman
illustrations by Shelly O. Haas

A Carolrhoda Creative Minds Book

Carolrhoda Books, Inc./Minneapolis

To Gina, Lisa, Theresa, Angela, Sara, Danielle, and
Claire, and to their dreams

B.A.

For Geoffrey
with special thanks to Tara, Alyssa, and Dillon

S.O.H.

Text copyright © 1997 by Barbara Allman
Illustrations copyright © 1997 by Shelly O. Haas

Library of Congress Cataloging-in-Publication Data

Allman, Barbara.
    Her piano sang : a story about Clara Schumann / by Barbara Allman ;
illustrations by Shelly O. Haas.
        p.   cm. — (A Carolrhoda creative minds book)
    Includes bibliographical references (p.   ) and index.
    Summary: Tells the story of the German pianist and composer who
made her professional debut at age nine and who devoted her life to music
and to her husband.
    ISBN 0-57505-012-9
    1. Schumann, Clara, 1819–1896—Juvenile literature. 2. Pianists—
Germany—Biography—Juvenile literature. [1. Schumann, Clara,
1819–1896. 2. Pianists. 3. Composers. 4. Women—Biography.] I. Haas,
Shelly O., ill. II. Title. III. Series.
ML3930.S385A45   1997
786.2'092—dc20
[B]   96-18217

Manufactured in the United States of America
1 2 3 4 5 6 – JR – 02 01 00 99 98 97

Table of Contents

① Debut

Clara sat near the window, peering through the lace curtains at the narrow street below. It was a chilly autumn day in Leipzig, Saxony—one of the German states—on October 20, 1828. Nine-year-old Clara was dressed in her best silk dress. She was waiting for the carriage to take her to her debut performance—her first concert as a professional pianist. She was to play a duet on the stage of the famous Gewandhaus concert hall. Her father, Friedrich Wieck, who was also her music teacher, had gone on ahead to make sure things were in order for her performance.

Leipzig, where Clara lived, was one of the greatest musical centers in Europe during the 1800s. In those days, there was no way to record music as it was being played. Because people could not listen to a recording again and again, a concert was an especially important event. People flocked to concerts to hear their favorite performers. The introduction of a new piece of music by a well-known composer was a much-talked-about and written-about event. And of course, when a new young performer, like Clara, appeared on the scene, concert audiences were eager to hear her.

When she saw the carriage turn the corner, Clara jumped down from her window seat and called to the housekeeper, Johanna, who hurried out from the kitchen to help Clara into her warm coat. As Clara climbed into the carriage, she could see neighbors peering from their windows with interest. Clara thought she was the luckiest girl alive to be on her way to doing what she loved—making music. Music had always been at the center of her life, and her father's training gave her confidence in her playing.

Not long into the ride, the carriage stopped to pick up other children who seemed to be dressed up for a party. Soon Clara did not recognize the streets they were riding along. She asked the driver why they weren't going straight to the Gewandhaus. When he replied that they were not going to the Gewandhaus but were on their way to a dance in the country, Clara panicked and burst into tears. The driver had mistaken her for another little girl in the neighborhood. Clara was in the wrong carriage!

At that moment, the driver of the Gewandhaus carriage pulled up behind the first carriage. Clara was rescued, but she arrived at the concert hall sobbing, shaken by her experience. Her worried father comforted her and tried to restore her confidence with his words of encouragement. Clara was able to calm herself. Even at the age of nine, she knew she must put all her discipline and concentration to work in her performance—and she did. That evening Clara played beautifully and without a mistake, and the audience applauded her warmly.

The next day, Clara felt as if she were dancing on a cloud. Father considered the concert a success, and Clara's name was even mentioned in the newspaper. In her state of delight, she sat down at the piano and composed a little waltz to cheer up Johanna, the housekeeper who had sent her off in the wrong carriage to her debut performance.

②

First Notes

Clara Josephine Wieck had been born into a musical family on September 13, 1819. Her mother, Marianne Tromlitz Wieck, was a professional singer and an accomplished pianist. Her father, Friedrich Wieck, was a respected music teacher who also sold pianos. Friedrich recognized Clara's talent and started her musical training early. He planned to devote much of his teaching career to Clara, knowing that her success would enhance his reputation as a teacher.

Clara was her parents' second child. Her older sister had died before Clara was born. Three brothers, Alvin, Gustav, and Victor, were born after Clara.

Not only did Marianne Wieck give birth to five children in seven years, but she continued to work as a performer and a teacher as well. Life with Friedrich Wieck was unhappy for Marianne. Friedrich was a demanding husband and father who always felt he knew best. To Friedrich, his own opinions were the only right ones. After seven years in an unhappy marriage, Marianne left her husband. It was an uncommon and very difficult thing for a wife to do in those days. People did not approve. Nevertheless, Marianne had left and had taken her children with her to Plauen. Before Clara was five years old, her parents were divorced.

Clara lived with her mother in Plauen for only a brief time. Her father insisted that Clara come home to Leipzig shortly after her fifth birthday so he could start her music lessons. He also took the two older boys with him. There was nothing Clara's mother could do about it, because by law, children were the property of their father.

It was very hard for Clara to leave her mother and baby brother. She loved her mother dearly. Being taken away from her made Clara sad. She had always been a quiet girl, but she became even quieter. This worried her father. In fact, she was so quiet that her father thought she couldn't hear properly.

Clara joined in group music lessons with her father's other students. She couldn't help but be excited about the music she was learning. As the months went by, she began to talk and laugh with her fellow students, just as her father had hoped.

Friedrich Wieck was becoming a well-known piano teacher. He was determined to make his talented daughter a concert pianist. He wanted to make sure Clara received the best training—and he felt that only he knew what was best for her.

In Clara's day, pianos were made with strong cast-iron frames and thick strings that gave them a brilliant tone. The piano's full name was *pianoforte*—meaning "soft-loud" in Italian. A piano could make very soft tinkling sounds as well as loud, booming ones. Musicians could play more than one melody at a time on a piano. And the piano was a perfect instrument to use when writing music—composers could play the notes of different choir parts or different instruments all at the same time.

Friedrich's teaching methods were new, and Clara learned quickly under her father's guidance. She practiced finger-stretching exercises and scales for strength and smoothness of playing. She learned to identify the keys by ear—naming the notes as the keys were played while her back was turned to the piano. She was taught to sing so that she could learn to give the piano a singing tone when she played. Clara learned that although a piano wasn't really built to hold onto notes to make a singing tone, a great pianist could make listeners *think* they heard it.

Clara was allowed to practice only up to three hours a day. Her father required her to spend time exercising outdoors every day to stay strong and healthy. She worked hard at her music to please her father. But her own talent, her sensitive nature, and her deep love for music made her want to learn all she could.

Clara's father started writing in a diary for her when she was seven years old. Journal writing, like letter writing, was an important activity in the lives of educated people of Clara's time. But because Clara wasn't old enough to keep her own diary at first, her father wrote what he thought she should write in it. If Clara practiced her music well, he wrote about it. If not, he wrote about what a lazy, stubborn, and disobedient girl she had been. When she began performing at age nine, her father wrote down details of her performances, the number of tickets sold, and her earnings. As Clara began writing in it herself, her father read what Clara wrote. The diary was one way that Friedrich used to teach Clara how to think, how to behave, and even how to manage her money.

3

Crescendo

As ten-year-old Clara and her father took their daily walk in the autumn air one afternoon, her head filled with plans. Next week she was to meet Nicolo Paganini, the great Italian violinist! Paganini was known and admired throughout Europe as a virtuoso—a master performer with a unique style. Clara knew it would be an honor to play one of her own compositions for him. She and Father decided on *Polonaise in E-flat,* and Clara was determined to work on perfecting it.

When Clara and her father met the great virtuoso at his hotel, Paganini invited Clara to play the piano for him. She was well prepared and confident, and she put her soul into her playing that day. The master was so impressed with her playing—especially with the feeling that Clara put into her music—that he invited her to come to all of his rehearsals and even arranged to have a special seat for her at his concerts. More than that, he treated her as a friend and fellow artist. When Clara asked him to sign her autograph book, Paganini wrote a section of music from one of his compositions in it. Clara treasured it. From the time of their meeting, she had a new confidence in her own musicianship. To have a great musician like Paganini for a friend gave Clara a new perspective on her own abilities.

Clara and her father traveled to Dresden, where she gave private concerts in the homes of well-to-do patrons of the arts. Not long after their return to Leipzig, one of her father's students, a young man named Robert Schumann, came to board at the Wieck home in order to continue his musical studies.

Robert Schumann was almost twenty years old— handsome, sensitive, and gifted. His mother had wanted him to study law, and to please her he had done so for two years, but his heart was not in it. He had begged to be allowed to study piano with Friedrich Wieck. Robert's mother had finally given in to her charming son.

Robert was eager to impress his new teacher, but not long after he began his studies, he injured his hand using a new device that was supposed to stretch the fingers for better piano playing. Robert was forced to give up his hopes for a performing career, and he turned to composing music instead.

Clara's home was a bustling place, filled with her father's students coming and going, as well as the sounds of the piano. Her father had married again, and her stepmother was busy caring for the children and a new baby brother.

Clara and her brothers loved to play boisterous games of charades with Robert. The frightening ghost stories he told them set them shrieking. In the evenings, Robert and her father's other friends often got together to perform in the parlor, and Clara was always there to play the piano.

Clara spent the summer of 1830 practicing for her first public concert as a solo artist. The concert that November was such a success that her father immediately began planning a concert tour to Paris. So Clara started to study French in addition to her other subjects. She practiced Chopin's *Variations,* a piece that many pianists found difficult to play well. Clara thought it was the hardest piece she had ever learned, and she worked at it with determination.

Clara and her stepmother, Clementine, packed for Clara's trip to Paris. At the top of Clara's trunk they carefully placed her new dress with its large, puffy sleeves and wide belt. It made Clara feel grown up to wear it and to arrange her braided hair into a bun on top of her head.

Clara was at an age when pretty clothes were becoming important to her. But her real reasons for being excited about this trip were artistic ones. Music mattered most to Clara, and Paris was the center of the artistic world. It attracted musicians, writers, and painters. Clementine's brother, Eduard Fechner, lived there, and he would introduce Clara and her father to people who could help her career.

On their way to Paris, Clara and her father stopped in the city of Weimar, where the famous writer Johann Wolfgang von Goethe lived. When the eighty-two-year-old Goethe heard about Clara's performance, he wanted to meet her. Clara and her father were invited to visit him. Clara politely sat on the sofa beside the old gentleman as they chatted. When he asked Clara to play for him, she sat down at the piano, but to her dismay she found she couldn't reach the keyboard properly. Goethe himself went into the next room and came back with a pillow for her to sit on. The great man complimented her bright and intelligent playing. Before she left Weimar, Goethe gave Clara a medallion and wrote a personal note of remembrance to her.

Paris was so different from home, thought Clara. Without Eduard's knowledge of the customs there, she and Father might be completely lost. Eduard had arranged for Clara and a French woman to go shopping, for Clara was told that in fashion-conscious Paris she must wear a different frock each time she performed. Even Father was done up in a new blue coat with velvet collar and brass buttons.

Clara realized that her father hadn't counted on the fact that Paris was full of pianists, including the flamboyant Franz Liszt and the talented young Frederic Chopin. It was difficult to be noticed, though Clara and her father attended many evening parties called *soirées* where Clara played beautifully on even the worst pianos.

While the Wiecks were in Paris, the dreaded disease cholera broke out. Many people left the city so they would not be exposed to the disease. To Father, that meant only one thing—there would be no audiences to hear Clara play!

Clara did play two small concerts. She also added something completely new to her performances that very few pianists did at the time—she played the entire program from memory, without reading from sheets of music. This required much more preparation on Clara's part, but it allowed her to concentrate more on polishing her performance. Audiences were impressed. After her concerts, Clara and her father left for home. They had been gone seven months in all.

On May 1, 1832, they arrived home. Clara was happy to be in familiar surroundings again. She tenderly greeted Marie, her new half-sister, who was just four months old. Robert Schumann had moved while they were gone, so Clara's brothers ran down the street to tell him the news that she and Father were home. Clara washed up, changed out of her traveling clothes, and was polishing knives in the kitchen soon after she arrived. Robert was excited to see his friends again and rushed over to hear about their travels. He wanted Clara to learn to play his new work—his second to be published—called *Papillons,* the French word for "butterflies." Robert noticed that Clara spoke German with a slight French accent. He thought the little girl had grown taller, prettier, and more self-confident.

Clara knew the trip had been something of a disappointment to Father, but her head and heart were brimming with all she had learned from her experiences performing and from her exposure to new customs and new people.

Yes, she would love to play *Papillons.*

Butterflies and Blossoms

In many ways, Clara had been treated as an adult throughout her childhood, because she was a finer musician than most adults. But as a teenager, she was experiencing the emotional ups and downs of an adolescent. She upset her father when she slept late in the morning. She cared more about spending time with friends than about practicing. Sometimes Clara rudely refused to answer when her stepmother spoke to her. Even her friend Robert noted that at times Clara's behavior was silly and childish.

Still, with Father's guidance, Clara grew as an artist. The first of Clara's compositions had been published in 1831—a collection of four dances called polonaises. Throughout the next two years, she played concerts close to home and continued composing. She studied music theory with a new teacher her father had selected, continued singing lessons, and studied French and English. Robert's compositions were also being published, and he relied on Clara to play them in her concerts.

Butterflies fluttered in the garden one beautiful morning in early August 1833. It was the kind of day that began with a soft, quiet promise of full summer. Clara sat at her desk near an open window with the pages of her newly published composition, R*omance variée,* before her. She had proudly dedicated this one to her friend Robert and intended to send it to him with a special note. Clara thought about how deeply happy she was because of the musical bond they shared. She wrote a playful apology for dedicating her work to him, and as she signed the note, Clara hoped her composition would please Robert.

In April 1834, a new student, Ernestine von Fricken, arrived to study with Father and board with the Wiecks. Ernestine was just three years older than Clara, and Clara was delighted to have her companionship. She didn't have much time to enjoy her new friend, however, before Father sent Clara to study in Dresden, seventy-five miles away.

Clara wanted to study voice and instrumentation, but she went to Dresden reluctantly because it was so far from home. She missed her family, and she was sorry to leave her friend and fellow piano student Emilie List and her new friend Ernestine. Clara wrote to her family often. She also wrote to Robert, teasing him for not writing to her often enough.

Robert was very busy. He was making a name for himself in musical circles by publishing a music journal, *New Musical Review,* that supported new composers and performers. Robert was the editor, and he wrote many of the reviews and essays that appeared in the journal. While he was encouraging the work of fellow musicians, he was composing his own remarkable music as well.

Clara was eager to make a trip home to Leipzig in July for the christening of her new little half-sister. It was a comfort to be back in the busy household she had missed so much and to see her friends again. But when she saw Robert and Ernestine together, it became clear to her that their friendship had deepened into romance while she had been gone. Clara returned to Dresden with a feeling of sadness.

Clara was back home in Leipzig by September. Early one morning, Clara awoke with a sense of expectation and excitement. It was her sixteenth birthday.

By six-thirty, Clara had already admired her presents and was prodding Father to get going. Why on this of all days was he taking so long to get ready? They were planning to meet other musicians at a restaurant in town for a celebration.

Just then a knock at the door announced Robert Schumann's maid. She was carrying a beautifully decorated plate with a present on it for Clara! Inside a little basket with a porcelain handle, Clara found a gold watch. It was a gift from Robert and from Father's other friends who would be at the party.

The birthday celebration lasted all day. There were flowers and a wonderful dinner. Though Clara was an artist who could communicate powerfully through her music, she still found it difficult to express herself in words at times, just as she had when she was a little girl. Even so, she gathered her courage during dinner and rose to her feet to give a small speech thanking everyone. After dinner Clara played for Felix Mendelssohn, composer and honored guest, who was also the new orchestra director at the Gewandhaus. And Mendelssohn played for Clara. In the evening, Father, his friend Dr. Reuter, and Robert Schumann took Clara dancing and for a walk afterward. For Clara, it had been the most brilliant of birthdays.

In the days following her birthday, Robert let Clara know his relationship with Ernestine was over. Then one evening in November, as Clara and Father were preparing for a short tour, Robert came to wish her well. When he left, Clara walked with him to the door, carrying a lamp. As they said good-bye, Robert kissed her—and she nearly dropped the lamp.

⑤

Seeking New Harmonies

Friedrich Wieck flew into a rage. He had not devoted his teaching career to producing a virtuosa so that she could marry and abandon her music! Robert Schumann was in no way suited to marry his daughter.

Even knowing her father as she did, Clara could not have guessed that he would be so outraged upon learning of her romantic interest in Robert. Robert respected Friedrich as his teacher and friend. But

Friedrich wrote a furious, insulting letter to Robert and immediately set out to keep them apart. He scheduled lengthy tours for Clara and forbade her to see or write letters to Robert.

Clara was deeply hurt by her father's actions and felt he was being unreasonable. She found his cruelty to Robert difficult to bear. Her heart ached, but because she was always an obedient daughter, she neither saw nor heard from Robert for the next year and a half. She continued to give extraordinary concerts and compose new works to play in them. All the while, she knew she could only be happy in a life filled with music—shared with the person she loved.

Friedrich arranged a concert in Leipzig in August of 1837. Clara stood up to her father and insisted on playing three of Robert's *Symphonic Études.* Robert attended the concert with a friend. After the concert, this friend helped Clara and Robert get letters to each other. Within days they were secretly engaged. But when Robert formally asked Friedrich to allow Clara to marry him, he was rudely refused. Clara began a struggle to become free of her father's control.

While touring, it was difficult for Clara to be separated from Robert. They wrote letters secretly. Clara could not even confide in her own diary, because Father still read it.

However, the welcome she got in Vienna lifted her spirits. Never before had she received such acclaim. Police had to control the crowds waiting to buy tickets to her concerts. At the local inns, her fans ate a special torte named for her. The newspapers praised her technical ability and the great feeling with which she performed. Music publishers fought over who would publish her works. The emperor and empress awarded her a medal and highest honors with the title of "Royal and Imperial Chamber Virtuosa."

Clara was thrilled by the success of her concerts. But with success and fame came the feeling that she owed much of it to her father, who had devoted his career to her. At times she felt ungrateful because she was going against his wishes in planning to marry Robert. Father had made it clear that if she married Robert, neither of them would be welcome in the Wieck household again. How could she turn her back on her father? How could he make this so difficult for her?

Clara was torn, and in a letter to Robert she wrote that music alone eased her heart. She put down her pen, sealed the letter, and sat down at the piano. Knowing that music could help her through the most difficult times, Clara began to play. And she played until she was near exhaustion.

Early in January 1839, Clara was on her way back to Paris, this time with a chaperone—and without Father. Heavy snow was falling, and fresh tracks were everywhere in the new snow. Friedrich expected the trip to be a failure, but he did not give his daughter enough credit. She had learned well the lessons he taught her.

In Paris, Clara gave successful concerts, made her own business arrangements, practiced, and taught. She learned she could manage without her father. Friedrich was angered by her success.

Robert wrote to her, proudly addressing his letters to the "Royal and Imperial Chamber Virtuosa Clara Wieck." He encouraged her to continue composing. He also suggested that she might find it fun to learn to cook and manage a household, and he hoped that she would not travel as much once they were married.

Clara did continue to compose. She wrote *Scherzo in D Minor,* which was very popular. And she put her soul into writing *Three Romances for the Piano,* dedicated to Robert Schumann. But as for Robert's suggestion about learning to run a household and staying home more, she wrote to him that she thought that while she was young and healthy she should earn as much as possible to help support them and his composing.

Robert sent Clara legal papers to sign so they could apply to the court for the right to marry without her father's permission. During their long and difficult legal fight, Robert experienced times of deep depression over taking Clara away from her father and the life she knew. But he also enjoyed periods of great creativity when he composed the first of his beautiful art songs—inspired by thoughts of Clara.

Clara and Robert shared a passion for the same ideas. They were part of an artistic movement known as romanticism. Like many other artists of the time—Mendelssohn, Liszt, and Chopin among them—they valued feelings and imagination in music. Romantic composers mixed musical ideas with poetry and painting. In his songs, Robert crafted the music to illustrate the deeper meanings of the words. In performing, Clara gave her music color, light, and shade, painting a picture for the listener.

Until she could marry, Clara went to live with her mother in Berlin. Clara and her mother grew closer during Clara's ordeal with her father—both women had suffered Friedrich's anger and overbearing actions. Months after applying to the court, Clara and Robert were granted permission to marry. On September 12, 1840, the day before Clara's twenty-first birthday, they said their vows in a little village church outside Leipzig. Clara wrote that after days of being hidden, the sun reappeared to bless their marriage as they drove to church.

Clara began a new chapter in her life, and she began a new diary with Robert. They took turns writing about their daily life as husband and wife. Clara wrote that those first months of marriage were the happiest she had ever known. In March she gave her first concert as Clara Schumann, at the Gewandhaus. In September 1841, the Schumann's first daughter, Marie, was born. On Clara's birthday that same month, Robert presented her with his new *Symphony in D Minor.*

Clara found it a challenge to fulfill her duties as wife and mother and still have time to practice and compose. She recognized Robert's need for quiet in order to write his music, and so her own time at the piano was limited. She was constantly frustrated with having so little time to practice. Remarkably, she still managed to give fifteen concerts in the first four months of 1842. Leaving the baby with relatives, Clara and Robert traveled together to Hamburg. Not long after they returned home, Clara considered another tour. After much convincing, Robert reluctantly said good-bye to Clara as she left for Copenhagen, Denmark.

Clara was treated with high regard by the Danish royal family, and she earned a good deal of money with her concerts. But Robert was miserable in her absence, and he wrote of his loneliness and despair in their diary. He also wrote that he did understand her need to keep on performing after all her years of hard work. Clara could not abandon the music that was so much a part of her.

Clara was proud of Robert's new oratorio, *Paradise and the Peri.* The choral work became a popular success when it was performed in December. It was based on the story of a fallen angel who is admitted back into heaven with the tear of a sinner who is sorry for having sinned.

At Christmas, after Clara's father wrote Robert a note of apology, Robert finally agreed to take Clara and the children to visit Friedrich in Dresden. Clara still felt greatly indebted to her father. She had given birth to a second daughter, Elise, earlier in the year, and she wanted her children to have a grandfather. Neither Clara nor Robert could put the past completely behind them, but they tried to make peace with Friedrich.

Clara turned to her wise and good friend Felix Mendelssohn for help in convincing her husband that she must accept an invitation to perform in Russia.

Mendelssohn understood that Clara was pulled in two directions by her need to continue her career and by her devotion to her husband and family. Robert finally agreed to the tour, and on January 25, 1844, Clara and Robert set out for Russia.

Clara enjoyed the trip, though it was cold and exhausting. They rode in sleighs across frozen rivers to get from town to town, and many of the inns were dirty and uncomfortable. Clara wore the pair of pretty fur cuffs that Cecile, Felix Mendelssohn's wife, had given her as a good-bye gift. She could slip them over her coat sleeves for warmth, and they were perfect for wearing on stage in poorly-heated concert halls, where the cuffs kept her wrists from becoming stiff in the cold.

In the middle of the trip, Robert suffered a mental breakdown, becoming ill and depressed. But he recovered, and they were able to go on to St. Petersburg. Clara's tastes had changed after studying music with Robert, and this was reflected in the programs she planned. She still played the showy pieces by Liszt and Thalberg that audiences expected to hear, but she also included her own preferences like Beethoven's *Moonlight Sonata* and *Appassionata.* She played her own compositions, Robert's *Piano Quintet and Variations,* and works by Mendelssohn and Chopin.

Clara performed for the czar and czarina of Russia in the Winter Palace, and she was named an honorary member of the St. Petersburg Philharmonic Society. Her Russian tour was profitable and successful, just as she had known it would be. It was time to return home to see her children.

6

The Perfect Language of the Soul

As Mendelssohn played the last notes of Beethoven's *Moonlight Sonata,* Clara savored them and applauded. Mendelssohn stepped down from the stage and escorted Clara from the audience back to the piano to have her play some of his songs. The occasion was a concert introducing the famous soprano Jenny Lind—the "Swedish nightingale"—to Leipzig audiences. Clara was delighted with the beauty of Lind's singing and felt her voice could fill any room with its soul. At a dinner party afterward, Clara discovered Jenny was a warm person as well as a great singer, and they became friends.

Since moving to Dresden, Clara had missed Leipzig's musical life. But family life and touring kept her busy. The doctor had recommended Dresden, known for its clean air and rolling hills, for Robert's health. Robert suffered tremendous physical and mental anguish. At other times, he still had periods of great creativity. To Clara, Robert was as dear as life itself. His mental illness was a burden that she carried bravely.

Clara's devotion to Robert's music was as strong as her devotion to him. During the times when he could work, Robert's music was still highly original and emotionally powerful. He depended more and more on Clara as a fellow musician. Clara assisted in conducting his choral group, helped in rehearsals of his larger works, and continued to play his piano compositions in her concerts.

Clara's family and responsibilities grew, and in addition she taught piano students. When she made concert tours to Vienna and Berlin, her dedicated piano student Emilie Steffens took care of the children and household for her. Clara was able to finish composing *Preludes and Fugues* and *Trio in G*

Minor. Clara relied on the discipline and devotion to work that she had learned from her father when she was a child.

To Clara and Robert, children were a blessing. She gave birth to Julie, Emil, Ludwig, Ferdinand, and Eugenie between 1845 and 1850. Emil was not strong and only survived a year and a half. The death of their baby son was a great blow to Clara and Robert.

To add to their grief, Felix Mendelssohn died suddenly in November. Clara felt a terrible loss. She had relied on her friend for his personal warmth and his great musical gifts. He had understood her need to continue her career after marriage, though it was not what was expected of a woman of her time.

When Clara was seven months pregnant with her sixth child, a political uprising in Dresden forced her and her family to flee to the outskirts of the city for safety. Rebels came looking for Robert to join them, but Clara knew he was too sick to help in their fight. Clara hid the younger children with the servants and escaped with Robert and their oldest daughter. She then returned home in the middle of the night, without Robert, for the younger children. While groups of armed men patroled the fields, she fled with her children to eventual safety.

Clara had always felt that the people of Dresden did not have enough appreciation or respect for Robert's work. Because he was writing larger works, he needed his own orchestra. So in 1850, she supported Robert's decision to accept a position as music director of the Municipal Orchestra and Chorus in Düsseldorf.

The people of Düsseldorf welcomed the Schumanns warmly, but Robert's illness continued to get worse. Eventually, he could barely meet the demands of conducting. His behavior was unstable, and at times he couldn't even bear the sound of music. Clara helped him with his duties and defended him against criticism.

Robert was still able to create music. He had never allowed Clara to hear his compositions until he finished them. When she finally heard his *Piano Trio no. 3,* it inspired her to write in her journal that her everyday cares amounted to nothing compared to the joy Robert's work and his love brought to her.

In 1853, when the family moved to a new apartment in Düsseldorf, Clara finally had a studio of her own. She was delighted to have her own music room on the second floor, far enough away from where Robert worked to allow her to play the piano without disturbing him.

Clara felt free and inspired again. That year she worked on her composing and completed four compositions: *Variations on a Theme of Robert Schumann, Three Romances for Piano, Three Romances for Violin and Piano,* and *Six Songs.*

On September 30, 1853, a handsome stranger from Hamburg knocked on the Schumanns' door. He had a letter of introduction from their friend the violinist Joseph Joachim and some of his own compositions tucked under his arm. Robert invited him inside and asked him to play. The young man had barely begun when Robert interrupted him and excitedly ran to get Clara so she, too, could listen. Robert and Clara were awed by their visitor's mastery of the piano and at the feeling and imagination in his astonishing compositions. His name was Johannes Brahms, and he was just 20 years old.

Johannes spent time with them every day for the next several weeks. Clara and Robert enjoyed his company as they walked and talked and played music together. This happy time reminded Clara of the early days in Leipzig when she and Robert were first caught up in the excitement of creating and encouraging new music. Robert published an enthusiastic article praising Johannes and promoted him in every way possible.

That November, Clara and Robert went on a concert tour together in Holland. Clara felt she was at her best and was thrilled when Robert, too, was honored publicly as he conducted his own works. For a brief time, the enthusiasm of their audiences helped them forget the criticism Robert heard at home.

The following February, Robert's illness completely overtook him. For ten days Clara stayed with him day and night.

When Clara stepped out of Robert's room for a few minutes to speak with the doctor, Robert disappeared from the house. Family and friends searched frantically for him in the rain. A short while later, strangers brought him home. They had rescued him from the river. The doctor felt it was best to send Robert to a private hospital, an asylum.

Clara received an outpouring of sympathy. Her mother, Johannes Brahms, and Joseph Joachim rushed to her side. The doctors would not allow her to visit Robert. At first, to her great sorrow, she was not even permitted to write to him—an echo of the sad times when she had been forbidden to write by her father. To Robert, music was the perfect language of the soul. While Clara was unable to speak to or write to her husband, playing his music was her comfort.

Three months after Robert's hospitalization, Clara gave birth to their son Felix. Clara had a large family to be concerned about. Her friends gave her support, but she did not want to depend on them for money. In her grief, she once again turned to music—her greatest comfort—to see her through. She began a heavy schedule of concert tours that took her throughout England, Holland, and Germany for the next two years. People opened their hearts and homes to her wherever she went.

Johannes Brahms was a true friend to her in these dark times, Clara thought as she finished reading his letter. Often he had put his own work aside to help her. He kept up Robert's household account books, visited Robert, spoke to his doctors for her, and wrote to tell her how the children were doing when she traveled. He was there when she needed him most, and Clara would always remember.

Clara was at last able to see her beloved Robert in the final hours before he died on July 29, 1856. Brahms and Joachim were with her at the small funeral. Clara prayed for the strength to go on without Robert, and she clearly sensed that his spirit was near.

7

Enduring Music, Enduring Love

Though Clara was absorbed in practicing, a smile crossed her face when her daughter Eugenie quietly entered the room and sat down to listen. Clara still began each practice session by playing scales, arpeggios, and exercises—just as her father had taught her. She moved on to pieces she knew from memory— Bach, Chopin, and Robert Schumann—and then to the new works she was learning. Eugenie often marveled at the freshness of her mother's exercises and begged her to write them down, but Clara changed them just enough each time to make that impossible.

As the years passed, Clara kept up her busy touring schedule during the winter months and rested during the summer at her home in Baden. It was a great joy to her to have her children with her whenever possible, even after they were grown. She continued her rigorous schedule of touring, despite the health problems that increasing age and overwork brought. Pain in her arms and shoulders sometimes forced her to seek rest at a spa where massage and mineral baths gave her some relief.

Clara continued to promote Robert's works in her concerts, just as she had done when he was alive. She felt it was important that people understood and loved his music for the innovative and beautiful work it was. Had it not been for Clara, it might have taken many more years for Robert's work to be appreciated. She did not want his music forgotten.

Though she continued to play her own music as well, Clara stopped writing major pieces after Robert's death. She had always felt her strength was in interpreting the works of others, rather than in composing.

Johannes Brahms sent Clara a new sonata. As she finished playing it, she thought no one could feel his music as she did—it touched her soul. During Robert's final illness, Johannes had come to care deeply for Clara. He felt she was the ideal woman—warm, intelligent, and a truly great artist. Clara knew Johannes was a generous, warm, and devoted man. She loved him for his genius and his noble heart. Clara was older than Brahms, and she had an established career and heavy family responsibilities. Johannes was a young man just beginning his own musical career. Together they decided their paths in life must take them separate ways.

Clara and Johannes lived at a distance from each other. As the years passed, they had their misunderstandings, and their friendship had its ups and downs. In their letters they shared practical advice about personal matters, finances, and family concerns. In sad times, Johannes's letters consoled Clara and encouraged her to have hope. She treasured the letter he wrote to her in later years that told her she was the one love of his life. Though Clara and Johannes never married, their love endured. Johannes was Clara's most important friend for the rest of her life.

Clara was the inspiration for many of Johannes's compositions, as she had been for Robert's. She introduced Johannes's new works in her concerts. And almost always, Johannes asked Clara for her comments on his compositions before publishing them. Clara accepted this job eagerly and was thorough in her critiques. She wrote that the joy his music gave her was impossible to describe.

In 1877 Clara took on the huge task of editing her husband's complete musical works for publication. She frequently wrote to Johannes for advice, and she worked hard to keep the music as Robert had intended it. Then in 1878, when she was approaching the age of sixty, Clara decided it was finally time to accept a teaching position and to travel a little less. She took a post at the Hoch Conservatory in Frankfurt that would allow her to teach and still travel when she needed to.

That same year, the school held a surprise celebration in honor of her fifty years as a concert artist. Clara was honored with a laurel wreath, speeches, and a special concert of her own works played by faculty and students.

Leipzig also celebrated her fiftieth jubilee. Clara performed at the Gewandhaus, on the stage where she had played her very first concert at nine years of age. As she walked onstage to perform Robert's *Romance in B Major,* Clara was surprised and delighted by a shower of nosegays tossed by the audience. The flowers were piled almost a foot deep, so the conductor had to help her clear a path to the piano. Clara was so moved by this reception that she felt herself shake.

Just as she had done fifty years earlier at her first performance, Clara calmed herself. She sat down at the
piano and once more dazzled an audience with the
passion and power of her music.

Afterword

Clara Schumann went on performing until 1891—thirty-five years after Robert Schumann's death and over sixty years since her career had begun. For many years, her daughters Marie and Eugenie lived with her, acting as her assistants. At age forty, Eugenie went on to a successful career in London as a piano teacher and performer, making her mother proud. Marie, Clara's oldest child, stayed with her mother as her friend and capable assistant.

Clara Schumann suffered a stroke in late March 1896 and died on May 20, at age seventy-six. Her devoted admirer, Johannes Brahms, wrote his last songs as Clara lay dying. Eleven months after her death, he too passed into eternity.

Recordings
of Works by Clara Schumann

Chamber Works by Women Composers. The Macalester Trio. Vox Box 2 CDX 5029.

Choral Songs for A Cappella Mixed Choir. G. Kegelmann. Heidelberg Madrigal Choir. Bayer 100041.

The Complete Lieder. I. Lippitz, D. Richards. Bayer 100206.

Complete Songs. Gabriele Fontana, Konstanze Eickhorst. CPO 999127.

Concerto in A Minor for Piano & Orchestra. A. Cheng, J. Falletta. The Women's Philharmonic. Koch International Classics 3-7169-2 H1.

Concerto in A Minor for Piano & Orchestra. V. Jochum, J. Silverstein, Bamberg. Tudor Records 788.

Concerto in A Minor for Piano & Orchestra. S. Launhardt, Z. Simane. Chamber Orchestra Merck. Bayer 100096.

Piano Music. Konstanze Eickhorst. CPO 999132-2.

Piano Music: Complete Works for Solo Piano. Jozef de Beenhouwer. Partridge 1129-2, 1130-2, 1131-2.

Piano Works. Veronica Jochum. Pro-Arte Records CDD 396.

Piano Works. Helene Boschi. Calliope CAL 9211.

Piano Works. Uriel Tsachor. Discover International DICD 920267.

Preludes & Fugues. Sylviane Defeme. CBC Records MVCD 1078.

Romances (3) for Violin & Piano. F. Biondi, L. Di Ilio. Opus 111 OPS 30-77.

Songs. K. Uecker, J. Polk. Arabesque Z 6624.

Trio in G Minor for Violin, Cello & Piano. Clara Wieck Trio. Bayer BR 100094.

Works for Violin and Piano. Olympia OCD 356.

Bibliography

Chissell, Joan. *Clara Schumann: A Dedicated Spirit.* New York: Taplinger Publishing, 1983.

Dowley, Tim. *Schumann.* London: Omnibus Press, 1984.

Frisch, Walter., ed. *Brahms and His World.* Princeton, NJ: Princeton University Press, 1990.

Harding, Bertita. *Concerto: The Story of Clara Schumann.* London: George G. Harrap & Co., 1962.

Latham, Peter. *Brahms.* New York: Collier Books, 1962.

MacDonald, Malcolm. *Brahms.* New York: Schirmer Books, 1990.

Neuls-Bates, Carol., ed. *Women in Music: An Anthology of Source Readings from the Middle Ages to the Present.* New York: Harper & Row, 1986.

Nichols, Janet. *Women Music Makers: An Introduction to Women Composers.* New York: Walker, 1992.

Pleasants, Henry., trans., ed. *The Musical World of Robert Schumann: A Selection From Schumann's Own Writings.* New York: St. Martin's Press, 1965.

Reich, Nancy B. *Clara Schumann: The Artist and the Woman.* Ithaca, NY: Cornell University Press, 1985.

Index